MIRACLES
Can Happen To You.

Power of
Visual Imagery

MIRACLES Can Happen To You.

Power of Visual Imagery

Lew Miller

Published by
MIRACLE PRESS
P.O. Box 99085
Louisville, KY 40299

Library of Congress Cataloging in Publication Data

Miller, Lew, 1917-
Miracles Can Happen To You, 85-61118
This book was formerly published under the title
Your Divine Connection, Card No. 77-79884
Reference: BV215.M5 248'.3 ISBN 0-89087-203-1

To my lovely and understanding wife, Jean

and our children

Mark, Doug, Greg and Becky

Contents

Foreword

THE MIRACLE POWER OF VISUAL IMAGERY

I'm convinced that your subconscious mind is your direct link with the all-powerful life force in the universe. You have an infallible Divine Connection with Infinite Intelligence, the wisdom of the ages, the secret that unlocks the creative process.

Through visual imagery, you can release the unlimited, untapped energies in the Universe. These magical forces will come to your aid to solve problems, improve your personality or health and guarantee success in any undertaking. It means you can be in complete control of your life not only when severely tested in the face of grave illness or danger but in meeting challenges in the everyday world.

It's a very natural but powerful mental activity that is sparked by vivid imagination, the most God-like faculty we possess. It's an active rather than a passive function. **Miracles just can't happen unless you expect (visualize) a miracle.** Being timid or fearful is not a part of the pattern. It is simply not compatible with unshakeable faith that is the catalyst in the divine creative process.

As you explore the techniques recommended, dwell often on this thought: Life is like a mirror; it gives back to you the reflection of your own mental image.

With deliberate, consistent use of the principles herein miracles can happen to you.

I

Lighting Up the Future

When I was eighteen years old I admired the dynamic producer Billy Rose who was considered by many to be the greatest showman of that era. I read about his theatrical achievements and felt an overwhelming desire to pursue a similar career.

Brashly, I wrote to Mr. Rose telling him of my aspirations and asked for his advice in getting started. Secretly, I was hoping he'd like my spunk and offer me a grand job working at his side in New York.

When his letter arrived I opened it with great anticipation. Instead, his advice to me was to get a solid college education with emphasis on economics, marketing, advertising and writing. He also suggested that it would be worthwhile afterward to sign on with a carnival, circus or tent show.

Tent show? It seemed ludicrous. They were virtually extinct. But, in a spirit of fun, I pictured myself in that carnival role. First I'd envision myself as a barker in the sideshow, then see myself as a roustabout swinging a sledgehammer driving in tent stakes or in a clown suit hawking cotton candy. Actually, I always considered the whole idea somewhat silly since it seemed unlikely it could ever happen.

Then World War II and a period of turmoil intervened. I was swept into it along with the rest of the country and millions of families endured many years of heartaches, separations, pain, deaths and broken dreams. Ten long years later many of us were still picking up the pieces and I found myself caught up in a most unusual set of career circumstances.

After my discharge from the army I could have returned to my prewar job with combination duties of traffic management, city sales and sales correspondent. Instead I elected to return to school with a career in advertising and promotion in mind. So far were my thoughts removed from the exchange of correspondence with Billy Rose a decade before that I never even recalled his advice as I registered for courses in economics, marketing, writing and advertising.

While still in school, I went to work part time as advertising manager of a new magazine venture. It was devoted to the vast rural electrification program. Because of shortages of personnel and materials during the war years the program had not made much progress and only a very small percentage of farms had electricity. Without electric power, farmers toiled from morning till night, usually with only the light from flickering kerosene lamps and lanterns. It meant endless chores for the farm wife who generally cooked on a wood stove, washed clothes with a washboard and carried hundreds of buckets of water each month from the well. Now a period of progress began that was to banish much of the backbreaking work.

The purpose of the magazine was to educate readers about the productive use of electricity on the farm and generally to further the program. In addition to advertising, I was also sent to interview and write articles about families whose lives were suddenly changing. They had not dreamed of some of the things happening in the homes they had known for years, oftentimes generations. Imagine switching on electric lights for the first time in the home in which you had been living all your life with only marginal illumination. Imagine a family's first lighted Christmas tree; the wife's appreciation of electrical kitchen appliances, running water and an indoor bathroom; and the delight of parents watching a child with his first electric train.

The excitement and enthusiasm that accompanies such progress inspires other ambitious programs. Soon I was engaged in a closely related activity that we developed to hasten our educational efforts. It was another communications vehicle to make the benefits come alive more dramatically than the pages of our magazine or community meetings could possibly achieve. We decided to take the story of electricity directly to the farm communities and provide education and information in an entertaining carnival-like atmosphere.

I became totally involved in establishing the format, organizing, publicizing and executing colorful two-day tent shows. They featured professional acts, popular country music groups, square dancing and friendly competition such as amateur nights, gospel quartets, beauty contests, cake baking and tractor driving. The winners, of course, received prizes, all of which were related to electricity.

There were very few ready-made fixtures which we could buy for a traveling show. We had to design and build portable equipment we needed. We hauled our canvas and bleacher seats on flatbed trucks which also provided the raised stage. Door prize drawing cages, exhibit platforms and lighting poles had to be custom made. Since it was a summer tour, we hired vacationing college students majoring in agriculture, dentistry, engineering and business. We probably employed the most intelligent group of roustabouts any traveling tent show has ever had.

Major manufacturers traveled with us and exhibited their products. Large groups would gather to watch demonstrations of cooking with electric ranges, methods of freezing and the use of modern kitchen appliances. Water pump distributors showed how to make a do-it-yourself running water system. Entire families would learn to use electric milking machines and electric pig and chicken brooders which would not only make their work easier but save the delicate lives of newborn farm animals.

I worked on advance publicity and promotion with newspapers, radio and some television stations. I hired professional entertainers, sold exhibit space and radio broadcast rights. We packaged entertainment segments and sold sponsorship and advertising rights. On a national level I lined up sponsors for the contests and managed them on the local levels which culminated in finals at the state fairs. It was the most challenging and, at the same time, most rewarding time of my life.

The rapid progress made in those years and the dawn of better living it afforded for so many who were denied those joys and benefits has to be one of the most glorious pages in American history. The leaders and farm people working together so vigorously to achieve their goal are in my opinion the outstanding pioneers of our century.

But what was a city boy like me doing in a place like this? My urban background certainly had not prepared me for rural life. The cares and concerns of the people who run the farms which provide the vital crops for our country were totally unfamiliar to me. I had never talked farm language before, but somehow I was now communicating with these fine people adequately. I was working with and speaking to 4-H clubs, Future Farmers and Farm Bureaus on a day-to-day basis.

It was only after the unique tent shows received nationwide attention that I recalled Billy Rose's earlier advice to me. Here I was caught up in the midst of this gigantic and thrilling promotion that was very close to what I had pictured a decade before, but only in the spirit of fun.

I realized then, there was a more startling aspect to my participation in this unusual scene. To that adverturesome and eager eighteen year old it would have been unthinkable to have seriously projected myself into such an unlikely career, particularly the romantic tent shows.

In those intervening years, however, my whole lifestyle and attitude had undergone a drastic change due to a series of extraordinary events that have had a profound effect on my life.

II

A Lonely Battle

During World War II, I was a platoon leader with the Fourth Cavalry Squadron, Mechanized, assigned to the First Army. After breaking out of the Rhine bridgehead at Remagen, we headed due east as did troops of the Ninth Army to the north. The mission was intended to surprise the Germans who were amassing along the Rhine in between the two widely separated crossings expecting we might try to secure that area first. Instead, we raced eastward and the enemy poured into the gap leaving itself open for one of the greatest encirclements in military history. We had been instructed to proceed swiftly and to avoid engagements and skirmishes. Heavy tanks and infantry behind us had the assignment of clearing-out the enemy where resistance was met. Our highly mobile reconnaissance vehicles were to keep moving ahead.

The next morning, just after sunrise, we were already twelve kilometers behind enemy lines. Our lead armored car was rounding a bend in the road. Suddenly, "Wham bang!" Its turret was torn off by a shell from a deadly German eighty-eight. A wicked weapon, the former antiaircraft piece was now being aimed at our advancing ground troops. It had the velocity of an M-1 rifle. We pulled back and took cover in the woods to the left as machine guns trained their fire on us from the heights to the right of our position. Sergeant Bob Knight sent word to us at the front of the column that Germans had felled trees behind us and we were trapped. Our scouts reported trees across the road up ahead but those were out of the eighty-eight's direct line of fire.

Now it was mid-morning. Our radios were jammed but the command we had been given was clear: "Keep moving. Don't bog down, keep moving." I knew that if we could maneuver around the felled trees, we might break out and try another route while support troops engaged the adversary. Seated at the machine gun in the jeep, I instructed my driver, Pfc. Pancho Serrato, to burst out of the woods around the barricade and zigzag down the road which would make us a difficult target. Our strategy was to send a second vehicle in the same maneuver as soon as the first disappeared from view. The plan would keep the enemy off-balance. It almost worked. We caught them by surprise as we darted out of the trees and my jeep was just about to reach a bend in the road where we would have been out of sight. But machine guns were trained on us from the hills on both sides and the bullets bit into the vehicle. We were both hit in the barrage of fire. Pancho was killed instantly by the gunfire and the jeep went out of control.

I caught five bullets; two in the head, two in the left arm, and one in the left shoulder. Thrown clear of the riddled jeep, I smashed against a tree and was knocked unconscious. When I came to, I was gazing into a bright morning sun and the grim faces of three soldiers from a German patrol. They picked me up in a raincoat and began to carry me over the rough terrain in the makeshift litter. My pain became even greater as I was bumped and scraped over the rugged ground. Sore and bruised, I was carried to enemy headquarters and deposited roughly on the hard floor. I was questioned again and again as I regained consciousness. Each interrogation was punctuated by the lifting of the shattered arm and letting it bang against the floor as the interrogator explained to his comrades: "Kaput." No first aid was given.

As night came on, the enemy had to abandon their command post when U.S. artillery began to zero-in on the town. The situation at the front was quite "fluid" and it was difficult for the Germans to tell whether the American troops were in front or behind. In their retreat, wounded prisoners were left behind. That was fortunate for me because the German medics did not have penicillin. There was no way my life could have been saved had I been moved to a German hospital in the rear.

For about one half hour, our artillery bombarded the town of Sassenhausen and the command post where I was being held. Tremendous bursts demolished walls and part of the roof. Debris rained down about me cutting and bruising my battered body. The pain was becoming unbearable. "My own side is about to finish me off," I thought in despair as I silently prayed for relief from the increasing pain.

Just then a cellar door across the room was pushed open and a German civilian stuck his head through and looked about. He spied me and apparently assessed my predicament. From below, he summoned help, and soon two German civilians appeared. They cradled me in their arms, and as gently as they could, eased me down the cellar stairs and into the basement rooms where the family obviously lived during air raids. They tried to clean and bandage my wounds. They fed me ersatz coffee or cognac which I promptly spewed up like a fountain. A woman bathed my forehead and wiped the blood from about my eyes. I wondered how many hours had passed. The shelling had ceased and attack troops were clearing the town.

One brave German civilian popped out of the cellar door waving a white flag at the attackers. Somehow, he made them understand he wanted them to follow him. Two riflemen, with a medic, followed the German warily into the basement. When they spotted me the medic shouted, "Sergeant, what the hell are you doing here?" He had served in Kansas with me when I was still a sergeant, and remembered me from that time. Since combat troops never wear tell-tale insignia there was no way he could tell I was now an officer. The soldiers recognized their officers by a vertical strip of adhesive on the back of the helmet, and non-coms by a horizontal strip. Quickly, the medic called for a stretcher and administered morphine for the pain. I thanked God for the blessed relief.

Sweet peace came over me as pain subsided; unconscious,

I was rushed to an evacuation hospital. Debridement of the wounds followed and operation after operation was performed as blood was transfused to replace the enormous loss from the gaping wounds. For twenty days, I remained unconscious while being fed intravenously. Finally regaining consciousness, I was aware only of my inability to move, to speak or to have any control over my body functions. I tried to see through blurred vision. I couldn't think straight and never really understood how or when I came to be there. I couldn't hear; it seemed voices were muffled or they reverberated as in an empty barrel. No sound seemed to be distinct. There was constant pain and a buzzing noise.

Month followed agonizing month with delicate cranial operations. Pain was undiminished and there was no gain in basic functions. Still having no control, I would lie there unattended, smeared in my own elimination and unable to communicate the dreadful plight. Paralyzed, unable to utter but incoherent words weakly, I was according to one neurologist a "museum of pathology." Even months later when placed on my feet by two attendants I was still unable to stand alone. My arms hung limply at my sides so heavy they caused excruciating pain.

The cerebellum had been partly removed along with a tablespoonful of gangrenous matter. There was considerable damage to the nerves in the head. The semicircular canal on the right was destroyed leaving me with no sense of balance. The cerebellum, the seat of basic functions learned as a child (walking, writing, word relationship), was unable to function. Relearning of fundamentals had to begin as with an infant. Reduced to this state, the knowledge of my condition seemed almost too much to bear. I had formerly had considerable physical strength and recalled with some pride how I had been referred to as an all-around athlete, with an uncommon degree of coordination. That I was making very little recovery hit me with sudden impact. It had taken many months before it finally sunk in and I came to terms with my physical condition.

One of the most painful of all the operations followed. It

was a mastiodectomy along with further debridement of the cerebellum. After many hours in surgery, I awakened in the recovery room, my shaven head bandaged tightly like that of an Eastern potentate. I was forced to hold my head in one position. The slightest movement in either direction made me feel as if my head had been jerked from its moorings. Consciously, I would hold my head in one position staring straight at the ceiling. There was a constant headache too. Coughing or sneezing would occur in spite of this and the pain became unbearable. There was agony and shock in simply having my bandages changed. It was even more frightening because I was unable to control my eyes. I wondered if this would be a permanent condition. The period during which I had to keep my head motionless stretched on for many days and sleepless nights.

Just about the time I was regaining a slight ability to move my head with a minimum of pain, I was taken from my room and carted off to what was a bizarre, unforgettable, maddening experience. I was being pushed into the center of an operating arena. I could make out the large, brilliant operating lights overhead. Peering down at the patient now on exhibition were dozens of inquisitive doctors. This was a medical seminar. The chief surgeon proceeded to explain my rare case and the nature of my grievous wounds. He treated the subject matter as if I were not able to hear or understand the medical jargon, and the highly impersonal nature of the questions. Due to my limited perception and faulty hearing it was certainly baffling at first. But as the long lecture progressed so did my awareness and it became totally degrading in my mind. Why was I being subjected to such utter humiliation and debasement? From that moment on I felt hostile, bitter and uncooperative.

Throughout this period I was also having ghastly nightmares, always about combat situations. I relived moments of horror in dream after dream. One recurring nightmare concerned our attack on the German town of Bogheim. My platoon was pinned down in a field under withering small arms, and mortar fire. It originated in buildings on the edge of town. To nullify it, our tanks began shelling them with round after round from their location in a wooded area at the right. Suddenly, I could detect through the fog that our tanks were moving out of their hiding place and mounting a direct frontal attack. As the lead tank rumbled into view, it received a direct hit from a rocket fired by a Panzerfaust (German counterpart of our bazooka). Flames shot high into the air and the buttoned-up tankers threw open their hatches to avoid being roasted. Screams of agony filled the air. It was horrifying to watch. So vivid was the scene, I could feel the intense heat as I viewed violent death about to happen. I would awaken moaning and screaming. My body would be burning up with fever, surely a natural consequence of my illness, but it generated the heat I felt so realistically in this recurring nightmare. Tense and frightened I'd pray not to go back to sleep.

Trying to communicate was the hardest part. I didn't know it then, but hearing was totally gone in my right ear and hearing was badly impaired in the left. Voices or sounds of any sort seemed to be indistinct and garbled. My vision was blurred; like looking through cheesecloth. Because of nerve damage my right eyelid wouldn't blink normally and tears streamed down my cheek. I was unable to gesture with paralyzed arms and had to rely on well-meaning orderlies and nurses to anticipate my needs, but they always seemed to "guess wrong." They brought bedpans when I was thirsty; they filled me with water when I wanted a bedpan. Every day I wallowed in my own elimination fifteen or twenty minutes before someone rescued me. The odor always reminded me of the awful stench of rotting human flesh I smelled in combat. That sensation would bring back the memory of decaying bodies or torn-off limbs giving off their putrid odors as they lay between enemy troops in a holding position. Other hospital smells triggered the memory but lying in my own excrement was mortifying and made keen awareness of the past unforgettable even for a few hours. My pride was bruised. I was ashamed and angry.

Another condition that plagued my mind was my inability

to breathe normally or regularly. Many times it seemed I just couldn't take one breath after another. Often, I had a sensation of being choked or suffocated. Sometimes, I felt I would stop breathing altogether. I would find myself gasping helplessly and laboring to keep alive before an alert nurse or doctor came to my aid with an oxygen mask. I had to rely on life-giving oxygen machines a dozen times in various stages of my hospitalization. I began to think I would never breathe normally again.

Eventually I became totally despondent and self-pity took possession of me. I cried softly, contemplating an endless depressing future; being consigned to a wheel chair, unable to run and jump, possibly unable even to work or raise a family. That was the pathetic picture I was making for myself. I could not detect any physical improvement and that added greatly to my tragic mental state.

Then another physical setback took place. My body, already reduced from a healthy one hundred ninety-two pounds to a pathetic one hundred and five pounds now began to wretch violently. Vomiting followed, and my eyeballs and skin began to turn yellow.

Yellow jaundice attacked and seemed dedicated to finishing the job. A week later, unable to take the kind of nourishment necessary to build my strength before any hope of recovery could begin, my frail frame weighed ninety pounds. I looked hauntingly like the photographs of the victims of the concentration camps. In a desperate effort to speed up nourishment, orderlies fed me four or five times a day, and supplemented that with malted milks almost round the clock. It seemed only to keep me from losing more weight in an offsetting fashion. Bitterness overcame me: any slight hope I had maintained was displaced by despair and fear. Even though I slowly pulled through the hepatitis, the labored breathing continued and I felt a sense of hopelessness. With clenched teeth, I was praying that God would let me breathe naturally and give me the strength just to keep hanging in there. That was all I could ask for the moment.

Terrifying nightmares again reflected my condition. In

dreams, I relived horrifying patrols in Hurtgen Forest. They always ended with our being hopelessly pinned down with no escape possible. Machine gun tracer bullets flew all about; mortar shells began to "whomp" in. Frightened and unable to move a muscle, I'd awaken overwhelmed with the reality of my own hopeless situation. Even in this state of mind, I was waging a furious battle to recover.

In the quiet of the long nights I would work myself over to the side of the bed, pull my legs over the edge and let them fall heavily to the floor. Straining, I'd try to stand. Since I couldn't hold myself upright without reeling I would simply fall flat on my face. The slight strength regained in the right arm enabled me to pull my dead weight (all ninety pounds) back up onto the bed. I would struggle with all my might to pull myself away from the edge and to arrange my shattered body on the bed. Exhausted physically, my sensitive nerves caused my whole body to tremble violently from the effort. I would lie there perspiring for an hour or so before troubled sleep would come. In the morning, my condition would seem worse.

Mentally and emotionally drained, I'd try in many ways to cope with the situation. I found that the harder I tried the more the problem seemed to grow in my mind. Realizing the mental aspects were even more painful than the physical injuries, I was ready to give up completely. The odds are against me, I thought. But I still managed to pray, begging for God's spiritual guidance because I was certainly making no headway at all with my strenuous physical efforts.

III

The Way Back

From the beginning I had been reciting *verbal prayers* over and over asking God to guide me in overcoming my infirmities. I had been pleading for help with such intensity and emotion that after each session I was utterly exhausted. It was only when I quit struggling and trying to conquer the situation through sheer physical effort that I began to find some hope and enlightenment. I made a personal vow to stop attacking the problem as if I were engaged in mortal combat with myself. In quiet meditation a few nights later I finally came to grips with the problems.

I was completely relaxed. My mind was emptied. Then, as if by divine inspiration, a procession of simple, pleasant and memorable scenes from the past began to invade my consciousness.

As a grade school student I recalled winning first place honors year after year. I pictured myself as I won a spelling contest and then first prize in a statewide essay contest. There I was, earning a scholarship to a private high school, winning academic and student leadership honors and being a proud member of championship athletic teams.

My mind became inquisitive, and as if engaged in some parlor game, I was being challenged mentally to identify the common ingredient that had spelled success in each instance. I tried not to concern myself with the material or physical aspects of the triumphs but rather was inspired to *dwell upon my mental state* in association with each event. Suddenly I realized that there was indeed a fundamental and common starting place in each of my successful ventures. Slowly, but clearly it dawned.

In *every* instance, *I had pictured that success beforehand.* When the mental image was particularly strong, it seemed afterward that the successful conclusion which was happening for the first time *had actually happened before.* Confidently, I had known beforehand it was going to happen. It was very much like an instant replay. The more vivid the picture and the greater the faith I had in it, the greater the degree of success. Whether others had regarded them as smashing successes didn't matter; it was my personal opinion that counted. That was the thought being projected in my mind. I began to think of other occasions when this same thing had occurred.

In basketball, I remembered picturing a strong mental image of the ball going through the hoop time after time. When I popped in six or seven long shots in a row it wasn't surprising. I pictured it would happen. I "practiced" seeing myself hitting a softball, driving in runs. When it happened, it was just as if it happened for a second time. I was able to improve my backhand in tennis with "beforehand" mental images. In the same way, I saw myself in reverie, days before a cross-country run finishing in the first ten in a field of three hundred and fifty top athletes. It happened.

Hadn't I envisioned myself leading my troops in combat? Although Officers Candidate Schools were filled with applicants and I did not have the opportunity of even attending, I had never let go of that mental image. Twice I had taken command in battle when we lost platoon leaders. Colonel Jack Rhoades conferred a battlefield commission on me in the very unglamorous setting of a machine gun post. An artillery shell exploding nearby bounced us unceremoniously out of the hole. Two days later, as platoon leader, I was headed for the Battle of the Bulge after the Germans had broken through in the Ardennes.

On and on, I recalled the successful incidents in my life and there was always one *single common denominator.* In each instance I had held in mind a *strong mental image* and clung to it with unbounded *faith.* Many times it was like looking at a motion picture and I alone was the audience. I had been doing this unwittingly all the time quite naturally. Suddenly, now I recognized it as a form of prayer. I realized for the first time that I might also use it consciously to share my problems with God when words were insufficient. This was the philosophy I would embrace for my recovery, I decided. After all, wasn't it simply that—prayers unencumbered with words?

Mentally I thanked God for the insight and for having brought me this far from death. I knew that all things are possible with God. By making mental images I was actually praying, communicating directly and clearly with God. I was making my consciousness receptive to His will and the life-giving substance to make it reality. I wouldn't concern myself with putting limits on God as to time of accomplishment or details and circumstances that would make it come into being. One can't dictate terms to God. But somehow, I knew, fundamentally, that it was my personal responsibility only to create the image and nurture it with faith. This was the stuff of which creation is made; it is the key to the creative process.

As I contemplated this, it struck me that *imagination is the most God-like faculty we possess.* What if my body didn't function normally now? Holding fast to a mental image of health and wholeness would change all that.

Immediately when I accepted this knowledge, this philosophy, a feeling of peace came over me. I was instantly aware of a sense of inner poise and power. I realized that God was expressing Himself in my mind and body and His divine healing was beginning to flow through my arteries, nourishing my mind and body. In fact, I pictured that it was doing just that and a warmth I never knew before seemed to animate my person. I knew full well that I would be guided to do all things to advance my recovery program. I envisioned that people, ideas and forces would be attracted to me to carry out the needed therapies and that it would all seem quite natural as it unfolded. In quiet confidence, I pictured myself daily becoming well and whole in every respect.

In a hitherto unknown state of relaxation I created strong

mental images that became more vivid each day. I saw myself walking, speaking in public to audiences, writing articles and stories, running, driving a car, raising a family, directing civic and charitable projects. I pictured myself on stage with entertainment activities, accepting business and social awards, and generally doing all the things that were almost unthinkable in my present physical condition. Each day I strengthened the images by visualizing still broader endeavors based on the same activities. In the morning, on awakening, I'd cling to the mental images with a glad heart. Before going to sleep, I'd picture them and thank God they were fulfilled. I delegated my problems to His divine power and thereafter began to sleep peacefully and naturally, without sleeping pills. No longer was there any strain, or worry, or tension. I experienced a spiritual awareness, an attunement with God that I had never known before. I felt an inner strength. For the first time, I knew what it meant that we are essentially minds with bodies and not the reverse.

Still nothing changed physically. The long, debilitating hepatitis had left me frail and pitifully weak. Yet it no longer concerned me. The pain even seemed lessened although it probably had not diminished at all. I was simply bearing up to it better due to the change in my attitude. There was no perceptible gain; no bright sign whatever. Still in quiet confidence and faith I developed my mental image of recovery, never doubting that it would materialize.

When you come to understand and pray through mental imagery as a daily practice, you are buoyed up by the knowledge that everything in the universe seems to be rushing to your aid to sustain you in mysterious ways. I was suddenly more aware of friendly small gestures, kind words, glances, strong hands, medical help, nursing skills and most importantly, love. All seemed to be working anew with great enthusiasm to sustain me in my crusade. It was a new song of life being skillfully orchestrated with every human instrument in harmony for my recovery; a concerto directed by the Divine Maestro.

New techniques suddenly were brought into play. In water

therapy, for example, my whole body would be suspended in a harness and then lowered into a tank of circulating hot water which stimulated passive nerves and muscles. With electrotherapy, paralyzed muscles in my legs, arms and face were being activated. Vigorous daily massages were given after heat lamps had warmed and relaxed inactive muscles. With each treatment, I visualized my body coming alive with life-giving spirit that I knew was coursing through my nerves, organs and veins. My mind was becoming keen and alert.

There was no instantaneous miracle but rather steady, dependable improvement. Gradually, amid much stuttering and stammering, whole words began to come forth. A victim of aphasia, I often said things not dictated by my mind. Words would be verbalized at random that I wasn't even trying to say. Most were indistinct mutterings. Speech therapists then taught me word formation using mirrors so I could see which efforts produced the desired results. They used tape recorders so I could listen to my own feeble efforts and attempt improvements. All the while, I pictured myself being congratulated for completing whole distinct phrases or complete sentences. Therapists encouraged me to sing along with the radio. The rhythmical style of the melodies made the words seem easier to pronounce.

Versatility in expression blossomed forth when I decided to try my talent at impersonations of popular vocalists of the day. I started with imitations of singing stars Al Jolson, Vaughan Monroe, Billy Eckstine, Maurice Chevalier and Louie Armstrong. Again, I used visualization by picturing their mannerisms, voice inflections and singing style. The mental imagery helped me to develop simple imitations certainly not of professional quality, but which provided social fun and entertainment.

This served to broaden my range, improved tonal quality and overcame my halting speech to some extent. Whenever I pictured the popular entertainers vividly and watched them perform on my mental screen I followed along without any hesitancy. My speech was not impeded one bit by the aphasia with which I was so often afflicted. As time went on I was even invited to sing numbers with amateur bands at hospital parties. I sometimes responded in a Vaughan Monroe or Louie Armstrong impersonation which seemed to delight the other patients and hospital staff. I soon found I could also do simple impersonations of Jimmie Cagney, Edward G. Robinson, Humphrey Bogart, Charles Boyer and John Wayne. A drama course I had taken years before with an obscure off-Broadway actor had taught me to visualize the character being portrayed for desired realism. These pursuits provided me with many hours of helpful speech practice and the diversion took my mind off my physical disabilities. In retrospect, the nurses and patients probably wearied of the whole thing since they were my primary audience, but they tolerated me and even cheered me on—sometimes.

Added physical strength preceded the next phase of my recovery. My arms and legs though somewhat impaired as to coordination at last began to take on flesh and symmetry. Although my left arm was still limp and heavy, I could lift the right one above my waist. With steady improvement, I was learning to feed myself. For a long time I couldn't hold on to the spoon or fork and had to learn dexterity. I was unable to "hit" my mouth every time. It was like teaching a baby to eat and it wasn't easily mastered. Perseverance was easier when I held before me a mental image of the full use of my arms.

The torturous nightmares continued but I had a new reaction to them now and the impact on my emotional state was lessened. I reasoned that these frightful experiences had not ended in disaster or I would not be alive. After each nightmare, I forced myself to remember the conclusion of each episode and would not allow it to end at a point of terror and helplessness. Each one now seemed to deliver a message and to give me added strength.

Still in a wheel chair, I was pushed daily to physical therapy, helped to my feet and propped up between the parallel bars of a walker contrivance. My legs would first be moved for me to simulate how I should step. It took several months for me to be able to take a few steps in the device. I was like a baby learning to walk. Besides, due to the severe head and cerebellar damage my native sense of balance had been destroyed. When strong enough to be able to walk by myself, I had to walk on a wide base to maintain stability. In negotiating corners, I would have to wheel around them to keep from falling. In going up steps I'd have to think about it consciously each time and estimate how far to raise each leg. There was no native recall to aid me since the cerebellum that largely dictates the procedure was so badly damaged.

In the dark or with my eyes closed I was without a reference point and unable to orient myself in space. I would always fall to the right. Direction of voices or other sounds was a mystery to me for I couldn't detect where they came from exactly. A tuning fork was used to demonstrate this phenomenon. Other tests on my feet and legs revealed that responses were just the reverse of what they should be. In spite of all these drawbacks, I was fully confident I would recover.

Once I had reached the point of communicating with the other patients and hospital staff I soon learned the greatest help in lightening a patient's burden was hospital horseplay. It was the great equalizer. It prevented anyone from taking himself too seriously. Similar antics perpetrated in a civilian hospital would be unseemly but in the army atmosphere it came off as uproariously funny. I remember a paratrooper with both hands amputated as a result of an airplane crash. Seating himself in a wheel chair he'd propel himself along with his feet. Coasting down the ward, he'd raise his stumps, gleefully shouting: "Look, no hands." Some patients would groan at the sick joke, others split their sides at this sheer craziness. Of course, he put on his act every time a new patient came on the ward. It surely took the edge off of things for many of us.

Switching bed tags on a new nurse was a popular pastime; she would spend days trying to figure out who got what medicine or which shots when. No one escaped! Often I'd be awakened by a patient after I had finally fallen asleep following a long wakeful period. Solicitously, he'd ask "Hey, Miller, do you want the nurse to get you a sleeping pill?" Much of a patient's leisure time was devoted to dreaming up pranks of some type.

My gags were somewhat tamer but they were in the spirit of the continuing game although not in the same style. When my paralyzed arm was beginning to show signs of regenerating, I delighted in telling my doctor I was worried I'd never be able to play the piano after my discharge from the hospital. "Sure you will," he said, attempting to console me. "That's funny," I replied. "I never could play one before."

As a result of this kind of banter, we originated a series for the bulletin board. I was beginning to practice using a typewriter to develop finger dexterity. Each day I'd type a "Joke of the day" or "Short, Short Story" and post it on the bulletin board. Throughout the hospital, nurses, patients and visitors would repeat the jokes or come to read them first hand. The lighthearted series (mostly one-liners) came to be called "Millerisms" and even today many who know nothing of my army hospital background use the same term to describe a style I developed then. It took a lot of research and effort to come up with a gem every day. This happy and creative period certainly was a natural part of the development that the All-knowing God fashioned for me in response to my visual prayers.

A new phase of recovery followed. I was allowed to travel on my own and urged to live free of family and friends to establish my self-reliance and independence. This was difficult since many times while attempting to order food or talk to a clerk in a store words would fail me completely. I would stand there unable to utter a sound. Embarrassed, I'd turn and leave abruptly. Back in my hotel room I'd envision myself in the same situation conversing freely and easily. Then I'd go right back to the same restaurant or store and begin anew. The words would come just as I had visualized.

Riding on jerking, swaying trains was my toughest assignment. Without my sense of balance I would fall all over the place while trying to make my way up the aisle of a moving train. As I staggered along the expressions of some passengers would register their obvious contempt and disgust for what they assumed was a drunken soldier. Many times I waited for the train to stop before moving from my seat because of my awkward predicament. Often I took a bus instead since rest stops were planned and walking down the aisle while the vehicle was moving was restricted by limitations of facilities.

At this time while on sick leave in Florida I suffered another setback. On the beach one day I had a terrible dizzy spell that caused the world to spin crazily about me for nearly twenty minutes. I could only lie there holding on to fistfuls of sand trying to anchor myself to the beach. It was all so frightening, moans and groans escaped. I'm sure those about me were frightened too. When the vertigo attack subsided, I was left with a feeling of nausea and a severe headache. Immediately, on wobbly legs I made my way back to my hotel room. I did not venture forth again that day but fortunately I was able to sleep. The next morning, I decided to go down to breakfast. There another attack began. I was seated in a chair and had to hold on tenaciously for fear of being thrown about the room. Again nausea and a headache followed. Thoroughly frightened by this time, I packed and took the next plane back to the hospital. I related the experience to my ward doctor who explained that it was to be expected from the severity of my concussion and the grievous head wounds. Since there was no way to predict when such attacks might start I had not been forewarned. The theory was that waiting in anticipation could instill fear and undo an otherwise satisfactory recovery. I never knew when to expect the attacks nor predict their length or severity. The doctor assured me the condition would eventually disappear. Actually, they continued for the next year before diminishing at all. It was nearly two years afterward that they had lessened to a point of little concern to me. Meanwhile, I thanked God it was not a permanent disorder and fervently pictured myself free of this mysterious malady.

Months later, I was finally declared able enough to receive

a discharge. My strong mental image of recovery had become a reality, my prayers had been answered.

But this was really a new beginning and it was strengthened by my now familiar practice of praying through mental imagery. I had observed so much suffering and deprivation, and this became a vital force in my transition. My strong desire was to do work that was socially and economically uplifting. I could see myself helping to bring joy and advancement to thousands but never concerned myself with the exact nature of the activity. Because I was learning to depend on divine providence, I would clear my mind and invite His will to take over. My recovery experience had taught me simply to hold out my hand and let Him lead me.

Lead me He did right back to college and also into the middle of the rural electric program. It was only then that I was guided in visualizing the traveling tent shows more vividly. It occupied my thoughts constantly because it felt so right at the time. I was soon involved in the wheeling and dealing of obtaining sponsors, booking entertainment, designing and building equipment and fixtures and transporting it from one community to the next, organizing and programming the tent shows and having the best time of my life before I realized that this too was a rerun of picture prayers I had visualized years before.

IV

Why Visualizing Works and How to Use It

After my very personal, and I believe, spiritually directed episodes, I did a great deal of spiritual and philosophical reading because I wanted to understand it better. It was so natural, I thought. Why wasn't it taught to us as children? Did intellectuals use it to their own advantage and did they all conspire to keep the secret from "average" people? I began to seek answers doggedly and found that they were *not hidden at all.*

Indeed, anyone receptive to new ideas can acquire it for his very own. You'll find it mentioned in scriptures, in novels, in daily news, in nature and even in the sports pages. Libraries contain good information on the subject.

The problem, however, is that you need to know what you are looking for before you can recognize it. It takes considerable research, discarding and accepting of ideas to synthesize all the facts and to devise a practical method that is likely to be helpful. That is very time-consuming and you will also glean a multitude of extraneous facts that can only confuse the matter. When you grasp the simple message you'll find a way to use it every day, not just when you encounter difficulties. To help you find some answers is my purpose in sharing my intimate personal experiences with you. Having been shown how myself it grieves me that others may be denied the same opportunity. Surely one doesn't have to suffer a great physical or mental impairment before being permitted such insight.

I first encountered the why and how of it in the scriptures. For the first time in my life I had begun to read the Bible with interest. I read in the hospital and from the Gideon Bibles in my hotel rooms while I was recuperating. Understand that I'm not a student of the Bible, just an investigator inquiring after the truth. I believe most Biblical passages are symbolic in character, not purely physical as some tend to believe. This is not intended to be a religious presentation but it is simply based on faith, faith in one's personal connection with Divine Power. I discovered that Christ said: "Whatever you ask for in prayer believe that you have received it and it will be yours." *Mark 11:24.** I've underlined the key words.

To "pray" is an attunement with the all powerful source in the universe. Thought, imagination, or mental imagery is the highest expression of prayer. Praying has nothing to do with the meaningless recitation of words but rather, praying is a spiritual thought process, most compatible with the spirit of divine thought when it is done in the form of mental images. To "believe" is to have complete faith in your prayer (thoughts). To believe that *you have already received,* you need only to visualize yourself as possessing it *now.* Belief in your mental image is the perfect expression of faith.

Stop a moment for here's a key thought. It will work either way you picture it. Your thoughts are forming and producing their physical counterparts continually. If you visualize poverty, and dwell on sickness and failures, believing those things are going to happen, they will materialize in your life. That's putting your freedom of will to work in the opposite way. God lets it happen because that's what you subconsciously prayed for. How often have you heard people say "I just know I'm going to have this difficulty or problem or that financial setback." They're visualizing failures; they're praying for it quite naturally. If you've been doing that yourself, you need to reverse your thinking or praying (change your mental pictures). It's the law of cause and effect. This example will over simplify how it works.

If you plant in your garden (mind) good seeds (constructive, successful thoughts, mental images) they'll produce nutritious fruits (success). You must of course water them with

*New Oxford Annotated Bible

faith and keep the weeds out of your garden (destructive thoughts weeded out of your mind). On the other hand, when you plant bad seeds (destructive, harmful thoughts, pictured in your mind) you'll harvest weeds (unwanted conditions in your life).

The practice is in effect what is called free will. Free will is simply your God-given right to choose your own thoughts and make your own decisions. The aching you feel to create and for personal fulfillment is shared by every person in the form of free will. If we strive to harmonize our own will with God's divine plan we become his agents, relying upon his guidance faithfully and depending entirely on Him as our source of creative energy and power. Freely will (visualize) what you want and God lets it happen quite naturally.

Christ said: "The Kingdom of God comes unawares. Neither will they say 'Behold here it is' or 'Behold there it is'; for behold, the Kingdom of God is within you." *Luke 17:21.* * Most people spend a lifetime looking in all sorts of exotic and lofty places. All the while, it's inside of each of us. We make our own heaven with mental pictures and faith (all within us) and we make our own hell by the same token. That's the key. It works in either direction. We are dealing with right thinking versus wrong thinking. The physical counterparts of the seeds we plant (good or bad) grow into our heaven or hell. Some day we may know all about it, but it occurs to me that "sin" as referred to in scriptures may just be wrong thinking. It is noted that before healing a person Christ often said, "your sins are forgiven you." He may have been, in effect, eradicating wrong thinking and reversing it to right thinking which preceded the healing. Maybe it was an instantaneous mental lesson transmitted so that the cripple had insight or complete understanding that his wrong thinking made his illness a reality. It resulted in extreme mental and emotional stress probably causing illness. Since scriptures were written in an abbreviated style perhaps a longer time-frame was required to reeducate the sick person to effect a healing. When

*New American Catholic Bible

you combine the use of mental images with faith, as in the proverbial mustard seed, it works quite naturally but appears to be miraculous.

Many will reject the idea as being *far too simple.* They will reason that in a complex world to solve complex problems the solutions must also be complex. That's the reason most solutions we try in this sophisticated world are seldom effective. They're much too complex.

Consider this. Are there some aspects of your life you would like to change? Have things not been going to your satisfaction? Have you been using a variety of methods to seek your goals but nothing seems to be working? If you consider them as unsatisfactory, wouldn't it be worthwhile to try this visualizing method to see if it can work for you? After all, haven't you given all the other methods, or no methods at all a whole *lifetime of your personal attention up to this point?* You'll never know if it will work for you unless you give it a try. There's nothing to lose. Even an incomplete effort can yield nothing less than an improvement over what is taking up time and space in your conscious mind now.

Upon first hearing the concept of prayer through mental imagery it sounds simple. What could be simpler than allowing yourself to daydream. Unfortunately, it is not quite *that* simple. There is a difference between just idly allowing your mind to wander and keeping it open, under control and receptive to only worthwhile positive thoughts. If you allow your mind to wander aimlessly it will frequently lead you to rehearse past failures and unpleasantness or, worse yet, project all manner of fears and anxieties. Uncontrolled thoughts like that can go on and on. If you want to learn to use mental imagery as prayer, this is exactly what you must *not* allow to happen. It requires self-discipline and persistence. It requires establishing and keeping in touch with your creator until His presence is with you—a constant source of strength—and you will need to draw upon it repeatedly to prevent negative thoughts from creeping into your consciousness.

A few simple exercises in this chapter are designed to help you establish new thought patterns and replace any old undesirable ones. To begin, first spend a few days or a week dedicated to the building of new thought patterns. If you've formerly embraced destructive, harmful thoughts (sowing weeds) and followed this as a way of life (except for a few rare occasions), you've probably developed very strong negative thought habits. That won't be easy to reverse overnight. The amount of time it takes will depend on the degree to which destructive thought patterns have become fixed in your nature. Now, you have to build a new thought pattern in simple ways.

Go on a mental diet of nothing but positive thoughts for two weeks. Picture yourself mentally thrusting out destructive thoughts when they obtrude on your conscious mind. Picture yourself forcibly kicking them out and welcoming only positive thoughts. See yourself vividly as being very cheerful in circumstances that ordinarily aggravate you. Be calm, waiting for a long stop light, calm in the presence of a person who normally irritates you, poised under what would ordinarily be embarrassing conditions. Repeating these routines again and again will establish new habit patterns. With this new you coming to the fore, picture yourself being admired for your pleasant attitude and calm, confident demeanor. Visualize your family and business associates responding even more favorably to you.

Condition yourself with positive, constructive thinking and learn by actually using mental images to change the basic you. It's that simple but it takes continuing perseverance. On the other hand, if you already embrace a positive approach in your life, you have a running start.

For mental conditioning, try this exercise. Before going to sleep, picture yourself awakening at 2:30 in the morning. You look at your bedside clock, recalling that you had visualized yourself doing this. Gratefully, give thanks for the ability you have. Then picture yourself awakening at your regular time in the morning, and doze off contentedly. Don't set your alarm. When you give absolute directions to your subconscious and dismiss it from your conscious mind, your subconscious takes over and awakens you precisely on time.

Be careful not to dwell on other matters. You'll clutter up the picture with too many items and it will be self-defeating. The key is to keep it simple.

Providing your own mental alarm clock is a fundamental technique. With it you learn the basic method for directing subtle, unfailing forces to work positively in your behalf. Relating to procedures involved, you must think of your mental activity as a two-part operation.

First, you have a conscious mind. You have complete control over your conscious thoughts. Remember, though, that it *can only do one thing at a time* and it works only when you are awake.

Second, you have a subconscious mind with such vastness, such power, because it is your direct connection with supreme intelligence. It is the wisdom of the ages and has access to all knowledge since the beginning of time. It can handle many thousands of problems and deal with thousands of facts at the same time. It works twenty-four hours a day.

The subconscious takes its direction from your conscious mind. Unfailingly and faithfully, it goes to work on the mental images and instructions it receives to create the physical counterparts in our lives. That's what happens in the simple experiment when you direct it to awaken you at a given time. For bigger challenges, it can call upon the most powerful forces in the universe. Like a great broadcasting station, it telecasts your message to all parts of the natural and supernatural world. It reaches all who are receptive, who vibrate to the same wave lengths of thought. In like manner, it receives answers from everywhere and anywhere on the topic or subject matter. Like a supercomputer, it analyzes, organizes, translates and communicates the powerful ideas to our conscious minds for action on the earthbound level. At the same time, it mysteriously communicates with other minds that can spring into action in your behalf. Like attracts like, and when your mental images are vivid enough in the inner world and held with intense faith, they will materialize in the outer world. You've heard it said: "I saw it in my mind's eye." That's mental imagery. Be single-minded when your desires are focused on the subconscious because your power goes where your attention goes.

For mental conditioning, here's another exercise to develop your ability to visualize. Close your eyes. Direct your attention to the center of your forehead. Imagine that there is a tiny screen you see there in the miniature theater of your mind. You are the only one in the audience watching the moving pictures being projected for your personal enjoyment.

Build the scenario according to some immediate goal or problem area you're having. Maybe it's giving up smoking completely, dealing effectively with a cranky neighbor, passing a tough examination, or starting on a diet to lose weight. Whatever it is, you write the script as it progresses, projecting yourself actively into as many successful, triumphant scenes as your imagination permits. Concentrate on it with burning desire. Then, turn off the mental imagery and begin to act in daily life as if you already had achieved that goal. Turn on your little theater performance whenever a moment of solitude presents itself. Your faithful portrayal of the role you're playing will cause it to actualize in your life in direct proportion to the belief that you have in your own theatrical production. The purpose here is to stretch your imagination and to become more accustomed to using mental imagery. From that start you can proceed to higher goals that may have eluded you until now. You can't give birth to an idea unless it's first conceived in your mind; visualization is the key.

Your subconscious mind is your true connection with the creator of life. When you learn how to use it, you're actually taking God as a partner in your life. Could there possibly be a higher calling in your life? God only wills for each of us (His children) health, happiness, love, peace and abundance. His will for us is constantly being expressed through our subconscious. When we desire and visualize for ourselves these same things, we are in tune with the infinite. We're letting His will work through us. That, I sincerely believe is the meaning of the phrase "Thy Will be Done." I personally experienced it, when I needed the health and life-giving love of the healing God to flow through my body for a full recovery.

My mental images and strong desires were not incompatible with His will for me. My conceptual prayer focused my will on a given result and allowed me to participate actively in the healing process. When I finally asked rightly, every force, idea and medical skill was brought to my assistance to actualize my pictured thoughts. There is a subtle connection between body and mind that we are only now beginning to understand.

With this mental giant working for you, you need never worry or fear. It arms you with confidence to act decisively and wisely. You can rely upon it implicitly because you possess the natural law of the universe. Your world is ordered according to your own thoughts and convictions. You can realize your full potential, expand your horizons and exhibit a depth of character others may find miraculous. When you begin to rely on the subconscious, you'll find the results can far exceed your expectations because you are stretching the imagination boldly and adventurously. With imagination, you can engineer your future. To do this, daily use of visual prayer (communion with God) is essential. Sincerely invite God to manifest His divine will through you.

God is everywhere present. You don't need special words to phrase your prayer, for God knows your thoughts and desires. "Pray to your Father who is in secret and your Father who sees in secret will reward thee." *Matthew 6:6.** You only have to turn your attention to Him, by creating mental images in your conscious mind, instructing your subconscious to take it forward, trusting it implicitly.

"Your Father knows what you need before you ask Him." *Matthew 6:8.*** This is creative prayer taking part in the innermost part of your being. You are in tune with the kingdom of God that's within. You are raising your spiritual awareness and harmonizing your thought pictures and your emotions with the spirit of God. You know that you can trust His will completely for His will for you is *only good.* Let the

*King James Revised and New Oxford Annotated
**King James, New Oxford and Catholic

great infinite spirit work through you and He'll teach you to do His will.

Using this natural law of God, your mind will attract to you only the conditions you desire. Your every thought is a prayer constantly creating after its kind. Knowledge that this principle is working for you should make you extremely happy. In that frame of mind, your mental conditioning will be accelerated. Even when you write or talk, try to use picture words or picturesque phrases. It'll instill in your consciousness, a spirit of thinking in mental images.

When and how can you use this new thought principle to maximum effect? Here's a method I've personally found productive. It's much easier for me when I use it before going to sleep and when awakening. Fifteen or twenty minutes is all it takes. These are specific procedures that might also work for you. First, ask God's guidance and sincerely invite Him to work His divine will through you in all your endeavors, then try these progressive steps:

1. Relax. Remove everything from your mind. Remember the conscious mind can only handle one thing at a time, so free it for concentration on one matter only.

2. If your topic is a special goal or a problem solving situation, dispassionately review all the facts you've collected about the matter. Regard it objectively as if you were reciting it to another person delegating the whole job of arriving at a solution. Now direct your mighty subconscious mind, supreme intelligence, to go to work to create the perfect outcome.

3. Visualize success and picture it vividly. See yourself happily noting the favorable results or successful outcome and perhaps having it be recognized and acknowledged by others. Treat only the outer conditions you want to be actualized. Don't try to work out the particulars, for that's the job of your subconscious. Trust that

extraordinary unseen forces are coming to your aid.

4. With unwavering faith, believe that it has already come to pass. See yourself already in possession of the satisfactory solution or desired goal. Act as though you have it now. It's the fire under the cooker that keeps it stewing and simmering in the powerful subconscious until the finished product is created. Then dismiss the matter from your conscious mind.

For me, that's the way the creative process works. I reinforce my mental images during the day while shaving, dressing, waiting for food to be served, as I walk along, in a movie, or just steal a moment before I start reading a paper or watching television. Even if they're only small mental bits, parts of the whole subject, it helps make the complete picture more realistic in the mind. Always be sure the mental picture shows a successful conclusion and *forget about the details.*

A word of caution. Never doubt for a moment that it will materialize. If you sow seeds of doubt, the subconscious picks up these thoughts and works on them and you'll get a cluttered, mixed-up outcome. A cluttered and confused mind results in a cluttered existence. As in the inner world, so it is in the outer. You'll be successful only in the degree you believe in your mental pictures. None of us ever uses the maximum amount of faith available to us. Ask God's help to install a new super-charged faith in your mentality.

A word about discretion. Don't discuss what you are doing initially. Many people cannot embrace such a simple, basic philosophy and would probably reject it at face value. Some might consider it for a while then not try it because of fear, worry, doubts, or maybe they're just not persistent enough to make anything work. These skeptics are the people who might ridicule you and destroy your successful initial efforts if you confide in them. Keep your efforts to yourself and your God. When you are confident about its use, poised and sure of your direction, then is soon enough to share your ideas.

One finds in discussing life and attitudes with people, precisely what type of individual will be receptive. You'll discover it is not wise to discuss it with a thorough-going pessimist although he or she is probably the one who needs it most.

The best way to reinforce your mental images is by daily periods of quiet meditation. Make it a habit to spend fifteen or twenty minutes each day in the quiet of your room, office or other sanctuary to rehearse the four-part method given earlier. The consistent repetition will help you to attain a higher spiritual consciousness that transcends the natural state and you are in close attunement with the infinite. This controlled relaxation slows down the physical self and causes the body to be calm and quiet. It relaxes the muscles. It relieves you of physical stress and mental strain. It has natural life-long benefits that are neither mysterious nor magical. You become more confident that divine resources are working in your behalf. It helps to create that personal inner poise and power that is a trademark of people who can deal effectively and persuasively with life. Considering the pressures and strains we experience today, the daily practice of meditation is vital.

It's not necessary, however, to take expensive courses in meditation which are the fad today. There's no need to master all sorts of mysterious chants and strange incantations to tap the inner reservoir of infinite strength and power. Simply do what comes naturally. Each of us is endowed with the innate ability to find the buried treasure deep in our spirit. Turn your mind inward to God.

I find it most conducive to meditation to lie in a recliner in a quiet room away from the beaten path. However you find quietness, you'll find inner strength and confidence. It is natural law. "But his delight is in the law of the Lord; and on his law he meditates day and night. He is like a tree planted by streams of water that yields its fruit in its season and its leaf does not wither. In all that he does, he prospers." *Psalms 1:2,3.**

*King James Revised and New Oxford Annotated

Don't overlook those moments of relaxation and leisure that can occupy the mind with other pursuits. Hobbies, recreation, sports, listening to good music, reading inspirational works, poems or the scriptures can be the time when the subconscious mind works feverishly on your goal or problem. Often the precise answers come in moments of relaxation or when the mind is otherwise occupied. We've all had demonstrations of this phenomenon.

Just keep it simple and remember that visualizing is a prayer form; it is your closest connection with divine mind.

Life is like a mirror. It gives back to us the reflection of our own mental image.

V

The Follow-Through

Once you have learned the fundamentals of visualizing prayer it can work to bring an exciting new dimension into your life.

With practice, you will develop the technique of painting pictures in your mind with the discipline of a trained athlete. You will learn to use it quite naturally and instinctively. At this stage, the habit of making mental images must become fixed in your mind through repetition and accepted as your new way of life.

Visualize for a moment a good athlete whether it's a star performer in tennis, baseball, golf, football or basketball. In baseball, you'll note that a batter doesn't stop his swing at impact with the ball. He follows through to give it direction and pace. It's the mark that identifies the skill that is associated with the smooth style and artistic grace of a real *pro.* By contrast, jerky, chopped-off strokes are characteristic of the inconsistent, inaccurate attempts of a novice. It's the follow-through phase that gives any endeavor in life the continuity that provides the momentum to carry it through to a successful conclusion.

Mental imagery as prayer takes daily practice. The suggested follow-through methods will reinforce and establish the concept firmly in your mind. The first follow-through exercise is to make an honest evaluation of your own imaging technique. That's the only way to correct purely selfish motives and to communicate effectively with God. Did you concentrate only on a single matter? Did your mind wander? How vivid were your mental images? Did you hold the pictures in mind with complete faith? Did any doubts assail you? Did you meditate on details or try in some way to direct your subconscious in the manner in which you want it to unfold rather than giving God a free hand in the undertaking? Directing it by giving all the particulars of how you want it done is, of course, counterproductive. Create your own mental scoreboard, and assign your own rating scale from one to ten, for example, in your critical personal evaluation. Visualize yourself as using this dynamic prayer power quite naturally *now.*

Dedication to good reading, especially the Bible, strengthens the mind and will. Read from a highly personal standpoint, imagining that the scriptures were written for you alone. The more joyous sections, the idealistic Psalms like the Twenty-third, "The Lord is my shepherd . . . " are uplifting and inspirational. Read the Bible expectantly and you'll chance upon many chapters that will teach you how to live life happily and abundantly. Invite God's intervention to learn what purpose in life He has for you. As you increase your spiritual awareness you raise your attunement with the Almighty and your follow-through becomes a graceful, well-directed swing into the future.

The diversion of listening to good music is an effective way to cleanse the mind and spirit. It can help fix the relaxed mind on a single subject. Listening to harmonious, uplifting melodies is like a musical bath. With the mind immersed in good music, higher vibrations have a way of soaking away our troubles and inviting beautiful thoughts into our conscious lives. With the higher thought waves, our minds become better receivers for tuning in on the continuing symphony of thoughts transmitted in the universe.

In like manner, an altogether peaceful and uplifting effect on the mind is achieved when we contemplate the wonders of nature and harmony in the universe. Feast your eyes on the simple miracle of a tree. Stare at the clouds, gaze at the stars, listen to a waterfall and drink in the beauty around you. During a rainshower, sit in the garage or carport and hear the rhythm of raindrops on the roof. It has a healing effect on the spirit. Sit on a park bench and watch the children at play or the squirrels or birds busy at their tasks. These are marvelous worry-chasers and you will feel closer to God.

Another exercise that will stimulate accelerated mental activity when you have a cranky problem to solve is using a *slant* or *incline board.* On a slant board, lie down on your back with your head at the lower end and your feet at the high end elevated about fifteen inches. I learned its worth since I was unable to pursue vigorous exercise or sports due to war injuries. I've used it regularly to stimulate circulation and to improve muscle and skin tone. I massage my face with my fingertips otherwise my facial paralysis is quite evident when the muscles sag. Using the slant board fifteen or twenty minutes a day will reverse the pull of gravity and take weight off your vital organs. Better still, it can give you a new "slant" on life.

It's not strange either that even the Holy Bible refers to rejuvenation when the Psalmist David blesses the Lord in his hymn of praise: "Who satisfied you with good as long as you live; so that your youth is renewed like the eagle's." *Psalm 103:5.** The key thought here is that the eagle that often lives for more than two hundred years, flies with its head lower than its heart.

Again, in sacred scriptures, relating his wisdom and understanding of many things, Job advises: "But ask now the beasts, and they shall teach thee; and the birds of the air and they shall tell thee." *Job 12:7.*** Animals do provide us with examples to follow. Keeping the head lowered is the practice of the long-lived tortoise, the crocodile and the opossum. The parrot, known to live hundreds of years hangs upside down from its perch. Dogs relax or sleep with their heads lowered.

The amazing Greek marathon runners renewed their energies by lying down at the foot of a tree and propping their legs up against it as high as they could reach. This position reverses the pull of gravity on the body. The glands are thus stimulated, the organs expand, and the body rebuilds and repairs itself. It relieves fatigue.

*King James Revised and New Oxford Annotated
**New American Catholic Bible

The nerve energy impulses are activated and as the blood supply and oxygen to the brain increases, *mental efficiency* is quickened. Experiments at Colgate University have verified that the brain function is faster and more accurate with the head lower than the heart. Mild exercises in this position on the slant board can be more beneficial than when in an upright position. More natural and deeper breathing is also encouraged. It can help normalize weight conditions by bringing body functions and circulation into balance. While doing this envision and invite divine energy through your subconscious mind to flow through your body, cells, glands, veins and organs to renew your body and spirits. Picture yourself as more youthful and vigorous. Mentally image friends complimenting you on your new appearance and sparkling health.

If you have some question about using this technique because of a personal physical condition, be sure to get your doctor's approval first. You don't need to buy a slant board! Prop your feet up on the side of a bed or sofa with your shoulders on the floor and head cradled in a pillow. Or, kneel down and rest your forehead on the floor, or sitting on a chair bend over with your head between your knees (either method is ideal when you feel faint). If you have good sense of balance, standing on your head or doing a handstand is even more effective.

If you question the worth of following such a program, consider the aging process. The great difference between old people and youngsters is mainly in the type of physical activity. When younger, we did somersaults, turned handsprings or cartwheels, played leapfrog, hung upside down from a tree limb, rolled down the hill, wrestled or engaged in rough-and-tumble sports where we were upended time after time. In these activities, the head was lower than the heart many, many times. When we discontinued those games as we grew older, deterioration was a natural consequence. You don't have to return to those rough-and-tumble days to slow down or reverse the aging process. Simply practice relaxing with your head lower than your heart. Try it a few minutes each day then gradually build up to fifteen or twenty minutes at a time.

As a supplementary benefit try this. When you sleep, lie on your right side without a pillow under your head, so your head is lower than your heart. The rejuvenation technique will work for you while you sleep. Since your subconscious mind does not sleep, be sure to give instructions to it before you fall asleep. It will help your mental images materialize more quickly.

The next follow-through exercise can release even more energies. Today, very few people breathe deeply. Our shallow breathing practices may indeed be the cause of poor physical and mental health of many people in this country. In comparable physical fitness tests, it is reported our youth does not measure up to the standards in most European countries. You might wonder whether it doesn't have to do with their hardier and sometimes more difficult existence. That may be true to some extent, but given our many advantages of superior diet, better health care, more recreational activities and superior facilities, shouldn't this difference be more than offset? Regardless, lack of deep breathing most assuredly is one of the deficiences in our health and mental practices.

Air surrounds us. It animates and directs the growth of all visible substance. Without air breathed into the soil and cells of the plant there can be no growth. This also applies to your body, mind, and your ideas that you call "inspiration." The dictionary defines inspiration as "drawing air into the lungs; the act of breathing in." As related to your mental activity, therefore, breathing in is required. As you breathe in air that is the source and substance of all life, knowledge and ideas, you breathe in the food and wisdom to sustain your body and mind. You thereby receive all the invisible ideas that take form in your visible world. Breathe in deeply, therefore, and envision with faith that you are consciously united with and surrounded by God's eternal wisdom, power, health, and happiness.

Since God is everywhere, He is present in the air which

you breathe. You should, therefore, be motivated to breathe more deeply to avail yourself of the all-powerful source. Do it as you walk, or drive, as you lie on your incline board, and certainly before going to sleep and upon awakening. Whatever is lacking in your life, see it instantly supplied and flowing to you in abundance as you breathe it in. You are thus cooperating with nature and the law of growth, the eternal fact of life. It also applies to the growth and manifestation of ideas as well as materializing along purely physical lines. Breathe in only God given thoughts: His inspiring ones, not yours. God's ideas are true and perfect, breathe them in—deeply, with the holy breath of life. The act of breathing then becomes a prayer.

How's your memory? Here's a follow-through technique that I've used as a learning method in public speaking. I make it a practice not to read from a written speech, or to use copious notes. A speaker should know his subject well enough to deliver an address without notes; otherwise the audience may not have much respect for his knowledge or competency. You can use this method for making a speech, preparing yourself for a meeting, interview, conference or school assignments. First, envision the character or makeup of your audience, and their interests. Then instruct your subconscious to provide you with a specific message or idea. Envision yourself embroidering that message with thought-provoking words and appropriate illustrations (painting pictures for the audience).

I find it helpful to write down the total concept as it is dictated to me by my subconscious, and then polish it in my personal style. Then, I dictate it into a portable tape recorder with precise pronunciation, rhythm, tonal quality, and desired emotional pitch and resonance. If I stumble over a phrase or word, I simply re-record. I don't want a flaw of some sort played back to me by my faithful subconscious mind, which takes over at this point.

I then lie down in a quiet room (or before going to sleep) and play back the recording over and over, visualizing myself giving the speech flawlessly. In the scene, I picture myself being interrupted with intermittent applause and am aware of the generally receptive attitude of the audience. I see myself being congratulated afterward by members of the audience, some of whom I may know by name. Understand that I never memorize. I simply instruct my subconscious on the matter, and have full confidence in that I'll be able to get up and deliver. "Now therefore go and I will be in your mouth and teach you what you shall speak." *Exodus 4:12**

You can do it for speeches or other subject matter which you need to learn. It will be ingrained deep in your subconscious mind and can be called upon at will. That is the objective of this particular exercise.

Service to others is the great immutable law that will help your life to yield its fullest and best. Give generously and unselfishly of yourself and your talents in the service of others. You'll discover many worthwhile causes in your community anxious to have volunteer workers, people who can lose themselves in the service to others. True greatness, happiness and fulfillment will never be found searching for it directly; it can only come indirectly as a result of helpfulness and kindness to one's fellowman.

Thoughts are a vital and living force. Dwelling earnestly on powerful thoughts, visualizing success-wishes, happiness and peace of mind for people, causes, and activities is also in the character of service to others. There are worthwhile causes just waiting for you to come forward and serve—youth programs, handicapped groups, hospitals, disadvantaged children, schools, community centers, recreational areas, all need you and you need them. The best way to get out of a hole yourself is to help someone else out of a hole. Thoughts and acts of help, love and friendship sent out and extended to others multiply themselves many times over.

As you expand your horizons with exciting new adventures in living, you'll find other people will be attracted to you in a rather mysterious fashion. An aura of magnetism seems to surround those who attain an optimum state of

*King James Authorized

awareness in this super-mental realm. Your own self-respect and confidence will be evident to others. Your ability to make decisions and to organize and direct your own affairs in an orderly manner will influence others to seek you out. Generally, they'll never express themselves as to why they came to you specifically, but they do understand intuitively that somehow you just might be able to help them. You become "special," and you're ready for the next step.

VI

Helping Others

Today, there are millions searching for "something more" in life. Maybe you can help someone facing a great personal trial to find the way.

As you reflect God's presence in your life, others will turn to you and you *can* help those earnestly seeking answers. You can offer your own experience to substantiate the power of prayer through visualization. You will be armed with the enthusiasm, poise and confidence that results from the experience of habitually praying through mental imagery.

You can explain the process and describe its use in very simple terms. Here are some ways to illustrate how we are connected with and are truly one with the source of all substance, wisdom, abundance and ideas.

The wheel is a very basic expression of our connection with each other and with the Almighty. The *hub* represents God and we, the people, are the spokes. One can readily see that the closer we get to God (the hub) the closer we get to each other. By the same token, the closer we get to each other, the closer we get to God. We become one with God and become in closer attunement with him, and other people. This is a principle of life that we merge with God and with each other as we attain this higher consciousness. If someone is expressing anger and bitterness with others, point out that the farther away he gets from others, the farther away he is from God. The answer here is to get close to God.

A simple illustration of how our thoughts spread out into space and how we attract similar thoughts from the ether can be demonstrated by the illustration of dropping a pebble, representing a strong mental image, into a pond. The waves it makes radiate outward in a circle much the same as our ideas radiate outward into space. Drop a second pebble into the same pond immediately afterward a short distance from the first and again the thought waves radiate outward from the center. These merge and overlap with the first thought waves and receptive minds record the ideas from space in a very natural way. Sensitive minds can pick up strong vibrations (thought waves), build upon them, add to them and use them to their own advantage. Similarly, others can acquire yours for their own.

Every day we place unquestioning faith in many material things. We punch a typewriter key and confidently expect it to print the symbol of the letter we pressed. In driving, we turn the steering wheel to the right with full faith that the auto will turn right. These mechanical devices in which we exhibit so much confidence are not one millionth as powerful as our subconscious minds, but we generally rely more upon them than we do the use of our super brain power. In the same way we press the typewriter key to get a desired result, we can press the right key with our conscious minds to direct our subconscious to deliver the physical counterpart of our mental image. It's important to understand this basic point.

Teaching it to young people is a vital phase in helping to restore man's dignity and self-respect in an unsettled world where traditional values and the very purpose of life is often being questioned. Respect for law and authority is being seriously undermined and public scandals, energy crises, vandalism, mounting crime, drug addiction and alcoholism add to our bewilderment and disillusionment.

Often people will ask you to pray for them when confronted with illness, personal, family or financial problems. I like to picture those for whom I am praying surrounded by a glowing white light of love and protection and filled with power, inspiration, health and abundance. Imagine that only good and positive thoughts and ideas can enter; no destructive thoughts can penetrate. When you put someone in God's protective custody, you have no reason to be anxious or concerned. When loved ones have serious operations, illnesses or accidents you can turn them over to divine protection in the same way. You don't need evangelistic zeal to help others find the way to dignity and self-respect. You do need the quiet, calm approach of a confident person who has great personal faith. That is the strength and the hope you can extend to others. Pointing them in the right direction and giving them a gentle nudge is the best assistance you can give. They, like you, must be self-taught and learn by doing. Those are the only lessons that "take hold" in our lives.

A most disturbing observation is that in this enlightened world with our advanced educational institutions we haven't scratched the surface with respect to the "scientific" use of the mind. In that area, we are still in a very primitive state as compared with the education we provide our youth in mathematics, physical science, engineering, history, medicine, and law. In our educational system, we neglect the most powerful, the most productive area of all, the realm of the mind. In our society, even small children know how to turn on a light switch or television set yet they have no understanding whatever of the principle of electricity or of transmitting pictures through space. Actually, they use these modern advancements with complete faith in the results they'll achieve. At the same time, we fail to educate them in the most useful, exciting, and powerful mind techniques that can serve them so well through life. This is unfortunate since youngsters are vastly *more receptive than adults* and prime candidates for grasping and using the principle of conceptual prayer. Their faith is unshakeable and they are still untouched by worldly adults who besiege them constantly with "you can't do this" or "can't do that." This is, unfortunately, the kind of pessimistic, defeatist world in which we grow up. In spite of this interference, children in their early years have unharnessed imaginations and strong beliefs and are more likely to succeed in this quest than adults. They are innately receptive to new ideas and ready for experimentation and adventure. Thus they are more apt and willing to try.

Scriptures express this fact beautifully. Christ recognized this when He said: "Unless you turn and become like children you will never enter the Kingdom of Heaven." *Matthew 18:3.** What do little children possess? The key to the Kingdom, a facility of making mental pictures and complete trust and faith in the outcome. They know how to use the life principle without strain or effort. Become child like and you'll solve your problems and reach your goals. Children approach life in a spirit of fun. It's that ability that helps them to be so successful in this venture of the mind.

Personally aware of this spiritual and educational opportunity, I've taught the fundamentals to my children. In their early years, they were able to demonstrate the laws of cause and effect quite easily and mostly without question. Each one has attained specific personal goals. Whether they've been academic, athletic, musical or social attainments, they've let me know how and when they've been successful. Sometimes they've let others know too. When my son Doug won a major junior golf championship at sixteen, he was interviewed by press and television. He was quoted in a newspaper as saying, "I just wish my dad could have been here because he helped me prepare for the tournament mentally. He convinced me I could win." I couldn't physically be with Doug that day, but my thoughts were with him.

Children are not born with fear; we simply teach them to expect the worst. It is a form of mind pollution. "For God hath not given us the spirit of fear, but of power and of love and of a sound mind." *Timothy 1:7.** To guide them closer to God's perfect will is the greatest legacy you and I can give our children.

*King James Revised and New Oxford Annotated

VII

Mental Pictures That Came to Life

Jim Thorpe has been hailed as one of the country's greatest athletes. Once he was on a ship headed for the Olympics. Other stars were running around the deck or exercising vigorously. The track coach spotted Thorpe, his decathlon entrant, sitting propped against a cabin with his eyes closed. "What do you think you're doing?" the coach demanded. "Just practicing," replied Jim. He then explained that while relaxing he was seeing himself successfully competing in his specialty. History has recorded his legendary feats and record-breaking performances. Jim Thorpe knew instinctively how mental images worked.

Monte Pearson, a major league pitcher, had a hunting accident that caused him to lose a leg. While recuperating, he envisioned himself pitching again in the big time. In spite of his artificial limb, Pearson did indeed pitch again in the majors. There are dozens of other comebacks similar to that in sports history and investigation would probably uncover that most of them practiced disciplined mental imagery.

Vic Wertz set many home run records when he was playing baseball for the Detroit Tigers and Cleveland Indians in the late forties and fifties. In August 1955, toward the end of his illustrious career, Vic was victimized by paralyzing polio. Fans speculated that he might be sidelined permanently. However, he made such a remarkable recovery that he was back in the lineup after only seven months, swatting them out of the park in his customary fashion. That outstanding performance earned him the distinction of being voted the comeback athlete of the year 1956.

Vic tells me that during his long illness he held a strong mental image steadfast in his mind, picturing his return to the game, still capable of hitting tape-measure homers. After Vic's baseball career, he entered business in Mount Clemens, Michigan. Years later, in 1966, he was honored with a national award for hiring the handicapped. During his illness, Vic had learned a valuable lesson about people needing people and he responded by finding a way to help others with special needs. Vic's career is testimony to effective use of mental imagery yet he says: "You and I know it; but who else will believe it?"

All right, you are probably thinking, those are some isolated examples that get extraordinary publicity because of the subjects' superstar status. How has it worked for you personally in everyday business and social activities you ask.

After seeing my mental pictures materialize in the magic of the rural electrification program and its traveling tent shows my next move was in the making. I was acquiring a flair for the dramatic, developing a variety of promotional skills, a sense of showmanship and absorbing important lessons for the future. That was the springboard to establishing my own advertising agency. This I had pictured while still in school and during my recuperative period. I developed a number of clients in the entertainment field including legitimate stage shows. During my hospitalization such an opportunity would have seemed impossible in my physical condition. It's quite strange too how our lives are touched by others as the drama of life unfolds. One of the star performers with whom I eventually worked was Vaughan Monroe; when I had been doing imitations of him years before, the possibility of such an association would never have entered my conscious mind. During this period I was also developing into a fairly well-known speaker, addressing clubs and business groups, and as master of ceremonies at dinners and banquets. I was invited to be on a half-dozen speaker's bureaus for civic and charitable organizations. My observation and imitation of top actors with whom I worked was most helpful. When I was regaining my speech, conquering aphasia, stuttering and stammering, I had been faithfully making mental pictures of myself as a public speaker. Back then, predicting I'd be comfortable in that role would probably have been termed by some as a foolish wish.

Great, you may be saying to yourself, but what about specific examples of how you tackled those personal activities one must face in everyday living.

Thirteen years after my combat injuries, I was still unable to pass a driver's test. Still I persisted in the practice of envisioning myself driving a car into my driveway. In the meantime, I was struggling along using taxis and busses for transportation in a business that demanded a much faster pace. Business calls and demands were not at all compatible with this restricting and undependable method of transportation. One night, a friend mentioned to me how much fun he was having driving one of the new compacts. Suddenly, it dawned on me that I was picturing myself driving a big, expensive automobile that I wasn't capable of handling. Immediately, I altered my pictures to feature a compact car suited to my limited abilities. Next, I discussed my situation with an auto salesman whom I persuaded to let me practice with a new foreign car. He agreed to let me develop my confidence on his lot until I felt I was ready, then use the car in the driver's test. If I passed, I promised him I'd buy his car. I began to picture myself passing the test. A month later I passed, and fourteen years after my war injuries I had my driver's license. My prayer pictures finally were answered.

I have built homes whose character and detail were precisely as I had visualized them years before. They included features such as a sunken living room, marble entrance hall, insulated windows and a raised fireplace. So exacting were my images that when we moved into that home, it seemed to me that I had been living there for years. I pictured a pool table in the basement of my home; it's there now for our use. On one occasion, in order to meet economic conditions, I developed a mental plan and picture of purchasing an apartment house, living in one unit and renting the others to meet our financial needs. It materialized just that way.

I use conceptual prayer to solve very ordinary problems with some imaginative twists. When my boys were small, I built an adjustable basketball goal and set it at heights relative to their growth and strength. This experimental idea led to a similar large project. For many years, I had wanted to construct a combination play area for my children but the fixtures I needed were either not available or prohibitive in cost. Calling upon my experience in devising special equipment for traveling tent shows, I made a mental image of the type of area that would be practical. I projected a dramatic moving picture on the three-dimensional screen of my mind showing my children at play in that playground. After two years of visualizing it spasmodically the whole project unfolded in my consciousness when we built a new home to take care of a growing family. At a minimum of expense I widened and lengthened the driveway and designed special fixtures and portable lighting for the asphalt area. I even designed portable backstops. Then we ruled it off with traffic paint as a combination playground for paddle tennis, volleyball, badminton and basketball. That playground has afforded many years of fun and entertainment for my family and their friends just as I had pictured it would years before.

My interest in writing stemmed from the articles and feature stories I had done for the rural electric program, and I took several courses in creative writing. Motivated to write I would select a popular subject, spend months researching it and reading everything available. Meanwhile I would visualize myself completing an acceptable story. I was actually directing my subconscious to absorb the facts, add its own vast knowledge and inspire me to write a finished piece.

Invariably, the creative process delivers the words, phrases and ideas in such a way that I actually write the story as though it were dictated to me. Many times it unfolds in my thoughts and I'm as amazed as a reader would be at a surprise ending. I've completed dozens of short stories in that manner. As I reread them years later I can never honestly remember having written them initially. This should not be surprising to people who deal regularly with words, ideas and concepts.

Ability to build an audience is probably the best test of the power of visual imagery. Supporting organized athletics has been of deepest interest to me in extra-curricular activities. Our local professional baseball team, a minor league franchise, had been the recipient of most of my devotion. At the time of this illustration, the team was in the midst of a tight pennant chase and its roster was composed of many future major leaguers. They included later Red Sox heroes and World Series contenders such as Carlton Fisk, Bob Montgomery, Lynn McGlothen, Rogelio Moret, Cecil Cooper, Dwight Evans, John Curtis, Rick Miller and Manager Darrell Johnson. Even with that roster the team wasn't drawing one thousand people per game. I undertook the task of a giant promotion to build a banner crowd. I pulled out every promotional and publicity angle in my bag of experience. I visualized every day for a month prior to the big night a filled stadium with overflow crowds lined up outside the foul line in the outfield. I could see the headlines and photo coverage as well as television and radio support. I told the general manager he'd be turning people away.

That night we had an overflow crowd of twenty-five thousand and the headlines and TV coverage were magnificent. It's recorded for posterity. The police estimated we turned away more than five thousand fans.

By mental prayer-imaging I have also learned to call on my inner resources to meet conditions spontaneously such as in business meetings or committee conferences. When a negative note is sounded by one or two people promising to destroy an otherwise desirable plan, I quickly visualize all being connected with the same harmonious, divine source. Silently, I send to the infinite power within me a quick visual-prayer picturing the dissidents reversing themselves and accepting the plan cheerfully. Other times, I've pictured another person speaking persuasively in behalf of a plan to save the day. Afterwards, they've confided in me that somehow a mysterious urge to speak hit them with specific ideas to voice that had not occurred to them earlier. Time after time, I've used that method in rural electric meetings to solve cranky sponsorship or prize matters. Often when dwelling on people at a distance, sending them mental messages to finalize a pending business matter, I've had these same people call me and express themselves with the exact ideas planted by the prayer-picture messages somehow transmitted through space. Coincidence, you say? Maybe so if it had happened only once or twice. When repeated dozens of times in various ways under different sets of conditions any conclusion related to mere chance has to be questionable too. Thoughts communicated through space is indeed a heady subject, but repeated personal experiences have convinced me not to write them off as coincidence.

If a person can relax and empty his mind without confused ends running amuck through his brain he can become both a receiver and transmitter. Extraordinary ideas and knowledge can come in this fashion and what is called ESP (Extra Sensory Perception) can and does occur. It sounds "spooky" but I'm sure many gifted persons can use ESP at will having trained themselves in the art.

Somewhere along the way you may question whether opening up new dimensions of the mind might not possibly be harmful. It's not dangerous to explore the efficient use of the mind. Indeed, it can be more dangerous not to. After all, God in his wisdom gave you that inquiring, searching mind. Use it.

No matter whether you believe in the idea of thought transference, you can be sure there is absolutely no mystery in how your mental images watered with faith can actualize for you in daily living. Believe in it and learn to use it. Dominant aspirations of the mind, vividly pictured as a form of prayer have a way of manifesting themselves by natural law.

By the way, I did begin visualizing over fifteen years ago that this book would be written and published.

VIII

Focus on Your Future

The central idea projected in this book is that thoughts are powerful forces that can build, change or revitalize man himself or his conditions. This is a principle as constant and dynamic as is the recognition that order in the universe proceeds from one source—God—the infinite spirit of life and power. All men who would seek truly great and lasting divine guidance must live in accordance with this law. This same law is at work in your life.

Like attracts like. A thought held steadfastly in mind (whether for good or evil) will actualize itself eventually. Anything must first be conceived in the *unseen* before it can be born in the *seen*. It is a thought before it becomes reality. The thought is the cause; materializing in the visible world is the effect.

Thought cannot be kept secret. It crystallizes into habit and then actualizes in the outer world for all to see. Good thoughts and actions can never produce bad results; bad thoughts can never produce good results. Bad results are the effect of wrong thinking and indicate the individual is out of harmony with himself. Since he is one with God and God's divine will for him is nothing but the best, his contrary force of will (opposing thoughts) is mental inharmony. Nature helps every man to gratify the thoughts which he most encourages. It never fails that your life responds to whatever thoughts are impressed upon the mind.

The body is a delicate instrument that obeys the operations of the mind whether deliberately chosen or automatically expressed. "A glad heart makes a cheerful countenance." *Proverbs 15:13.** Sickly thoughts express themselves in a sour face and weak body. Anxiety quickly demoralizes the body and invites disease and illness. Strong, pure, happy thoughts build a vigorous, graceful body. Your thought habits will produce like results. Why dwell on physical health? A healthy body depends on and reflects health of mind. Your body is the instrument of God's creative expression of life on earth. Man as a complete entity also relies on harmony and balance of bodily functions for its balanced thoughts and emotions—mental health.

No one can prevent you from choosing your own thoughts. Maybe you feel you didn't choose your present circumstances but if you persist in the same train of thought that brought these conditions about you'll never shape new and better conditions. It is this ability to choose your thoughts that can be described as your own free will. By merging yours with God's will (Thy Will be Done) you can attain to all the abundance, peace and happiness that He wills for you. When you make yourself receptive to the wisdom and guidance of universal mind you become one with the purpose of God. I believe each of us is identical in quality with God, our source, the same as a drop of water taken from the ocean is identical in nature and characteristics with that ocean, its source. Christ said, "And the glory thou hast given me, I have given to them that they may be one even as we are one; I in them and Thou in me; that they may be perfected in unity." *John 17:22.**

When we hear that we're created in the image of God, that likeness referred to has no reference to our physical bodies. That resemblance, I believe, refers to our ability to function in the invisible mental realm and exert similar creative powers. The imaging faculty we possess is what marks our Godlike resemblance. We have the responsibility to develop that ability and unharness the vast God-given intellectual capacities that lie hidden deep within us. Those who explore those depths of thought and subtle mental and spiritual forces will develop in the image and likeness of God.

*King James Revised and Oxford Annotated

You may object that you have no right to exalt yourself in such a way. On the other hand, if you believe you are one with God and emanated from that divine source, you fail to glorify Him if you don't allow His will to manifest itself through you as an extension of Himself. Each one of us is very special to Him. We have a contribution to make that no one else can duplicate. We've been empowered with a free will to actualize the things we desire. The divine will is constantly at work within each of us, guiding and urging us upward by our thoughts. When our thought forces are *spiritualized by mental images* and *firmly believed,* they become thousands of times more dynamic and powerful. The drawing power of the mind in such a state possesses vital, creative energy and is the most irresistible force in the universe.

Review again the steps to prayer through mental imagery. Form a strong mental picture of what you desire, then see and believe you are already enjoying or experiencing that condition. Unforeseen help will spring up along the way when you cling steadfastly to your image. The initiative is yours. Start now, persevere courageously and believe. There's magic in believing. You have only to make the start. Something in the universe responds to brave, intrepid thought. Faith and courage have magnetic power in them.

God knows your needs completely. When you paint a bright picture of your desire and frame it with beautiful sincere faith, it becomes God like in expression and materializes in the exact degree of your belief. Using thought-pictures is praying in its highest form. It unlocks the mighty hidden powers within you by virtue of the divine creative principle. The practice of repeating pictures throughout the day (offered in faith as one works) is prayer without ceasing. Making such pictures creates emotion and even helps encourage a stronger spiritual bond between ourselves and our Maker. Pictures are worth thousands of lifeless, barren words. Language is often a barrier because words constrict conscious thoughts and place limits on understanding. Words appeal primarily to the senses and cannot accurately describe spiritual, emotional non-verbal communication. The higher spiritual state of mental images transcends language. Every man has to discover truth for himself and it can only be known by direct experience not someone else's description. Books and teachers can give you the information but only through your personal use of this knowledge can you gain wisdom and understanding.

As you pray in this manner, do not struggle to attain faith. We often hear the admonition to "pray hard on the matter." The tension and doubt associated with "praying hard" is self-defeating. Learn to *pray gently.* That attitude implies absolute faith in the outcome. To put your total confidence and belief in it, pray in a relaxed state of mind. The more calmly, quietly, expectantly, you pray, the greater your belief is expressed. When you pray gently, it indicates you expect your prayers to be answered.

There's still another practice that can be self-defeating in prayer. Sometimes you may feel disappointed and discouraged that your prayers are not being answered. You may feel hurt and unhappy that your sincere efforts are not being rewarded. This may be the hindrance. You may be trying to work out the details in your own way, trying to force matters on your own terms with the notion that you are the one who can make it materialize. In a sense, you may be blocking the creative inflow that is so vital to the outcome. You're just possibly twisting your divine connection into a knot stopping enlightenment and guidance from flowing freely and abundantly into your being through the proper channels. At such a time, you must learn to surrender to His divine will; then let go and let God take care of the matter. Trust Him implicitly. When you entrust Him with your burdens and problems you must give Him an open channel to express His highest good through you. Remember always as you pray: let go and let God assume His creative role. Don't interfere by trying to do it your way.

Here's another thought that can work wonders as you pursue the habit of right-thinking. Sometimes "unwanted" things seem to happen in our lives. Hardships, misery, suffering, illness and debts are manmade yet some choose to think they were visited upon us by divine providence. People will state they certainly didn't desire them.

This is the time to stop and reflect. Regardless of whether you think you brought it on yourself, here's an opportunity to learn and profit from a lesson in understanding. When things go right in our lives we customarily praise and thank God for our good fortune. When fear-laden situations come into our lives, use the same practice: give praise and thanks for what you consider "unwanted" and for what you may not be able to understand at the time. Direct your thoughts toward the Infinite Spirit and express your lack of understanding. Let God know that you can't possibly recognize the advantage in it but that *you have complete faith* in that it's for a greater good. Communicate your full confidence in a happy outcome and repeat your praise and thanksgiving with a sincere heart and mind. As you glorify God in this manner, the miracle power takes over. It isn't the situation that matters but how you view it that's important.

Trials and hardships frequently unlock men's greatest virtues. Nathaniel Hawthorne once lost his job and thereupon reported dejectedly to his wife that he was a failure. She wouldn't "buy" that appraisal and encouraged him to develop his writing skills with the blessing of the additional spare time he now enjoyed. The result: he worked more effectively and turned out "The Scarlet Letter," and followed it with other masterpieces. Many great works of art and musical compositions were born out of suffering and deprivation. Lives of Beethoven, Milton, Dante, and Cardinal Newman are classic examples. Learn to give thanks and praise whenever trials or grief come your way. Lose yourself in your work; it's the greatest therapy in the world.

There is a great spiritual awakening about to break through the fear-laden theories about a vengeful God who punishes people with all sorts of misery and chastisements. Divine mind is stirring in the hearts and thoughts of men and women everywhere. I believe the greatest advancement in history will be seen in the next fifty to seventy-five years by sensational discoveries in the realm of the mind, especially in its efficient use.

Although we may only be scratching the surface compared to those revelations to come, you can be assured that you now have the means to tap vast hidden powers within you. Pray with visual images, earnestly believing and seeing that they have already happened in your life. It's the secret Christ gave us when He promised, "Whatever you ask in prayer, believe that you have received it and it will be yours." *Mark 11:24.** With a firm grasp of the principles you can start to use prayer through mental imagery now in every phase of your life. You can exceed the highest ideals you might have wanted for yourself heretofore. God created you to express His infinite good. Whatever you can conceive in your mind can be achieved. Believe in yourself and focus on your future with enthusiasm and self-confidence.

May God bless your life and your efforts to glorify and praise Him in this worthwhile endeavor to improve conditions for yourself and others with mental imagery, your Divine Connection.

"Do not be conformed to this world but be transformed by the renewal of your mind, that you may prove what is the will of God, what is good and acceptable and perfect." *Romans 12:2**

*King James Revised and New Oxford Annotated

Lew Miller and son, Doug, enjoy a game of pool. The author, former Supervisor of Promotion for General Electric Company, is active in entertainment programs for school, church and social organizations as well as Speaker's Bureaus. He and his wife, Jean, are the parents of one daughter and three sons. They are long time residents of Louisville, Kentucky.

* * *

The author is compiling unique success stories of others using the methods recommended herein. He invites you to write to him, in care of the publisher, relating any personal experiences you have had with either the deliberate use of mental imagery or achieved automatically by instinctive use. Please include written permission to use as presented, or edited subject to your final approval, in published form.